Thorn Ki…

Poems from English Battlefields

By Clare Mulley

The Battlefields Trust

For my family, and the students and staff of The Hampshire School, Chelsea.

Published in Great Britain in 2016 by

The Battlefields Trust

29 Wolseley Road, Godalming, Surrey, GU7 3EA

Copyright © The Battlefields Trust, 2016

www.battlefieldstrust.com

Registered Charity No 1017387

ISBN 978-0-9956304-0-6

Contents

Foreword

The Battlefields Trust is the only organisation with the core mission and national remit of protecting, interpreting and promoting the battlefields of the United Kingdom as historical and educational resources. As Winston Churchill famously said, 'battles are the punctuation marks of history', and a study of them can help us to understand our nation's social, cultural, economic and political development.

Poetry has a particular role to play in examining the importance of battlefields as special locations of human conflict and endeavour. It can help to foster insight, empathy and a recognition of the common and often acute human emotions of valour, fear, triumph, sacrifice and loss experienced by those caught up in the battles fought on them. In writing these poems about the battlefields she has visited and experienced in her unique role as the Battlefields Trust's poet in residence, Clare has made a very special contribution to the work of the organisation.

I commend these remarkable and moving poems to you.

Howard Simmons
Chairman of the Battlefields Trust

Four key English Battles

Hastings, East Sussex, 14 October 1066
Harold Godwinson's English army occupied a strong position on Senlac Hill but were eventually worn down by the relentless attacks of William of Normandy's cavalry, infantry and archers. Harold and his two brothers were killed.

Towton, North Yorkshire, 29 March 1461
The largest and bloodiest battle of the Wars of the Roses. Fought in a blinding snowstorm, Towton saw the crushing defeat of the Lancastrian supporters of Henry VI by Edward IV's Yorkists. Large numbers of Lancastrians were slaughtered in the rout that followed the battle.

Bosworth, Leicestershire 22 August 1485
Richard III was defeated and killed by the forces of Henry Tudor who went on to rule as King Henry VII. The intervention of the forces of the Stanley family on the side of Henry was a key moment in the battle.

Naseby, Northamptonshire 14 June 1645
Parliament's New Model Army, commanded by Sir Thomas Fairfax and Oliver Cromwell defeated Charles I's and Prince Rupert's Royalists in the decisive battle of the English Civil War.

Introduction

The following poems were inspired by four major battles – Hastings, Naseby, Towton and Bosworth - and the last few months have seen me getting sunburnt at re-enactments, trying on armour, reading poems over loudspeaker to gathering 'armies', tramping miles over country lanes, pushing through wheat fields full of nettles, sploshing through mud and puddles, drinking a bit too much mead and hitching lifts from my ever-patient and enthusiastic friends at the Battlefields Trust, all in order to get a bit better acquainted with some of the landscapes which shaped our history. I've seen so many sites which hold memories of some kind, often sad, often grim, sometimes even funny, and explored some of the most beautiful countryside in England. Needless to say all this has inspired a lot of writing.

I wanted to write this work for several reasons, the first being that battlefields, and particularly the lesser-known ones, don't always get the recognition they deserve. This is partly because some of them aren't easy to locate exactly; documents of the relevant periods don't always contain the clues needed to pinpoint one piece of land. There is also the inescapable fact that they are just that - fields. A listed building has the advantage of being something unmistakeably solid which you can restore, wander through, and enjoy a cream tea in after viewing the architecture and furnishings. Ask the average day tripper if they'd prefer to see a stretch of grass where there was most likely a battle, or the still-standing manor house where a famous nobleman lived, and you can bet what their answer will be. Most people prefer to search for the traces of where others like them existed day to day, because there is always something comfortable in similarities. While this, at least, is understandable, many also fail to see the significance of what a battlefield actually is. A piece of ground where armies fought under horrific conditions and died in their thousands - ground which may still contain those thousands of human remains. So many sleepy rural backways and quiet corners conceal sites like these, which at the very least deserve our respect, but often go unnoticed due to lack of other local interest or funding. Worse still, local councils, who would throw a fit if anyone tried to dig up even a corner of the village graveyard, are often quite willing to build on battlefields, favouring 'development' over the preservation of something which should be protected by default. Bosworth and Hastings now have very attractive and educational tourist centres which do a lot to redress the balance, and Naseby is in the process of creating one, but there is still a great deal to be done elsewhere. It seemed a good idea to write something which might help raise awareness, however small, and inspire more respect for these sites.

For a long time, I have also been fascinated by the strong links between battles and land, both in the sense of how they formed the England we know today geographically, and the physical relationship between the natural world and combat. On the one hand, battles were once the means to an end, cloaked in all the trappings of their end results. They helped to form dynasties, cultures, religions, literary genres and economies, triggered quirky life stories and anecdotes by the bucketful - who can forget the eccentric image of Prince Rupert riding into battle with his poodle? - and provided the backdrop against which the futures of entire countries were gambled. On the other hand, there's no getting away from the reality of what they were, after all the political planning and niceties were done. A battle, though 'organised', was by the end a mêlée in which creatures made of flesh killed and hacked at other creatures just like them, leaving a mass of torn bodies for the birds and animals to pick at and miles of bloodlogged soil.

I've often wondered how wildlife would react to battles, if it had a voice. The scale of slaughter was sometimes so great that entire ecosystems were affected by it; the flooded Cock Beck near Towton is said to have run red for days with all the bodies which fell into the water. All this comes alongside a horribly practical angle which most people have never considered – ironically, while planning this large-scale slaughter, leaders had to choose terrain according to bodily needs. There had to be enough water to sustain men and horses, and enough food supplies nearby, which meant grabbing anything you could lay your hands on, at the expense of local peasant farmers. Men often had to provide their own armour and weapons, and improvise if they didn't have any. If their side lost, they had to run wearing pounds of gear. While we're on the subject, where did armies go to relieve themselves? The answer: wherever they possibly could - most battlefields essentially became open-air latrines. It's easy to forget details like these when studying history, and when so much of warfare is still glamourised in the popular media. Whatever you're doing, and however noble the cause, you can't escape the grime that comes with being human.

Those filthier human undertones are the main reason why I was inspired to write these poems. I'm not specifically a war nerd, and wouldn't choose to spend my whole day constructing model armies or discussing tactics and weaponry, interesting though it all is. I also find it amusing that people seem to focus on royal families and the nobility, who really only drove the machine, and whose ancestors they are so ready to resent. The element which really fascinates me in terms of battle is ordinary people - their beliefs, their fears, and how they reacted under extreme circumstances. There is a terrific clash between the animal instinct for combat, which I think everyone has in some measure, and the more cultivated instinct that violence is wrong, and this in itself provides a huge amount of material. Obviously it doesn't do to generalise; you could write whole books about the extent to which the natural desire to fight wins against general squeamishness and the desire for peace, and how living in different historical periods might have affected this balance of desires.

However, I think it's safe to say that the majority of people don't, and didn't, spend their lives having to kill one another face to face, and that getting into the mind-set for doing so is no small feat. How would they have coped? How would we cope if we had no choice, and, if we weren't the ones fighting, what would it be like living next to a combat zone? My great grandfather used to 'forget' his bayonet in the trench before going on sorties, and risk being court-martialled, because he couldn't bear the idea of stabbing someone. He would have been labelled a coward by many at the time, but I often wonder how today's society would view him. Seeing what we are (literally) made of as opposed to what we are in our heads is not only humbling but nauseating, and even, or maybe especially, in an age where death was more in the public eye, it would have been a terrifying prospect. A great deal of art and literature around the late Middle Ages in particular, when the Black Death was at its peak in Europe, depicts a morbid obsession with decay, showing that people found the juxtaposition between the ethereal beauty of the soul and the all-too-corruptible body both fascinating and very hard to deal with. Not much has changed, it seems.

With all this in mind, what I ended up writing in a nutshell was a series of poems about what battlefields really are, the wildlife found on those battlefields and, above all, how the populace might have seen and related things if they could speak with us today. I don't pretend for a moment to know what any of them really went through, but I hope it gives visitors food for thought as they stand on these sites, where so many ordinary men and women once faced the unspeakable.

Clare Mulley
Wandsworth, 2016

The Forgotten

Songs are of Kings, but battles are of men;
the creatures of the field and by-lanes
tongues steeped in the rich sod that they must steward
but can never gain, following where the herder leads
and bought and sold like sacks of grain.

So when you cast your thoughts to crown and heritage
spare one for them, the multitudes ordered to practise on a Sunday;
the Toms, Wills and Hals down by the village butts,
praying they'd never draw a bow and hear the hiss and thud
as the barb sank itself in something other than the target's wood.

The Crow

I, *corvus corvus*, the devourer of blue-eyed and brown
red-haired and grey - each and all leavings, as I must -
can't help these shoulders, hunched as eaves against life's storm,
nor unslant my squint, window to the world's charnel house.

Man can but seek windfalls, play God and petty dunghill King
with the too little ground, the littler lives afforded him;
so who is he to point the finger, to despise such ones as I?
Not all gifts are welcome ones upon this earth. We all must die.

My business is the funereal, the hidden banquet of the field
after the pageantry, the gathering in of banners, trampled flowers.
Someone must make a living of the dead. Someone must make dead
of those once living and now sung, no longer ours.

Stubble Dreams

I am spread-eagled with my spine to the roots of a tree creaking with the voices of dead birds. The shaven ground mourns a millennia of sap choked in before completion. This is a scape of flat things, cut-off edges, borders. Through the back of my head I sense another skull tilted to the boughs. Caught in his last grimace, he laughs derisively at the way of things. He is my shadow. I feel his thumb pads prick my own. He tells me not to believe any of it, la gloire. He tells me to get used to being meat. Sod jellies in his eyeholes, earth's richesse burgeoning upwards in a mush of shoots and furs.

He

He's coming. Him across the sea.
He says we're liars and he'd know
a liar. He's got the wrath of God.
He's building ships, he's sharpening
his spear, his star burns white-hot
above our villages. They say
the Pope is on his side, he's got
the banner to prove it, and
a massive sword. Some of them
higher up the ranks have whispered
that they won't protest, that he will
make our country great, and slipped
him notes, winking. He has

commissioned tapestries. He
doesn't play the game. He'll wait
till you're off sorting out
another skirmish, then catch you
sweating after miles of road,
his armour polished, not a hair
gone cockeyed, smelling strongly
of rosewater. The bastard. He's an adder
in the apple cart, a weasel twisting
on unbloodied grass. He'll turn
the other side of that long face
and run downhill into the marsh
then turn again when we give chase,
thinking we've won. Some say he

is the pious type, that he will build

a monument over our bones

and weep, his gilt mouth birthing

lyric after lyric in a key

more beautiful than any gone

before. He will tear apart

our words and build a tongue

which sings and cuts. He's looking

to the North, already slavering

to purify her wastes, he

uses fire like farmers use

a flail to thresh the corn.

He is the Devil. He is glorious. He

is as tall as centuries and young

as borderlines on waste ground. He

has made his destiny and found

that God never says 'no.'

Far out at sea, the timbers creak,

bringing him on. He'll

burn our messages of peace

and hang our emissaries

at his gate. It won't be long

until he's hammering on our doors.

Our hour grows late. Our children

shudder in their beds. Tomorrow we

will climb the hill, and wait

and wait.

At the Watershed

This is water's meeting place
where velvet blades give way to fleshy stalks
where fleshy stalks give way to deep loam
where loam gives way to moss
and moss collects sky's sacrifices into mottled bogs
bled from the saturated high grounds to fall
stuck through with reed spears.
The ripe cloud line bruises under its own weight
 and piles, ready to be crushed, the stratosphere throbs;
soon growth roads will vein each plump hillock
each hidden trough
running running running
and still more
it will overflow the ditches, the land will swell
cushioned by wet, overfull with it,
rimmeled on stricken ponds, burst from wellsprings
in the endless woods. It is only right that life
should both gush and sink here.
Horses sense it, across laden miles,
a darker print upon the wind,
and the parched men
take each blessed gulp for what might be their last
of this birthland of damps and dross,
half-lit wilds where things fall to mulch, glistening.

The Facts of Life

There is nothing between the soul and heaven
but air.

There is nothing between the soul and air
but bone.

There is nothing between the air and bone
but flesh

There is nothing between the bone and flesh
but blood.

There is nothing between the flesh and blood
but seconds.

There is nothing between the blood and seconds
but metal.

There is nothing between the metal and seconds
but your own hand.

Hymn for the Dawn

It is the hour before the light delivers us from dreaming;
in consciousness of flesh soon to be tested
all cares shrink to this hushed field, and to God.
God in the rising damp
God in the hoar-encrusted wheel ruts
God in metal's answer to the morning
dully sheened, a muffled clarion of pheasant in the wood,
the clattering of wings mocking our swallowed urge to fly
anywhere but here
here in the face of God
where none can prepare us for the sullen brightness of our blood,
the shrill of armour meeting, or that man and woman
scream at the same, slaughterhouse pitch
when opened.
Sing we now our canticle of Bearing -
the heavy pikestaff, brutish shield,
arms of our fathers, groans of our mothers,
weight of man on wife
to bring the heaviness of children
to bear arms once again –
for how shall we endure, if not through song?
My sons, my daughters, take up your harps, feel
The wealth of blood fall from them
ingot-heavy, wine-rich, ringing -
your dank earth's inheritance.
Ora pro nobis, domine; we are not made
to last, or know our limits.
Brothers, let us lie down and contemplate our father, Ground;
we live only for returning.

The Ambush

They had skirted the hedge, looking all the time for the softest path
free from betraying twigs. Somewhere a horse
   whickered at silence, the smell of it

                        pressed down
              and there suddenly
the others, standing twenty breaths' distance.
The moment rounds, grows pendulous,
               a water bead
hung on the grass that fringes them, as yet untrampled -
   yards away, one lad yawns,
another tosses ribaldries, unsure of how to fill an instant
both eternal and long lost (not knowing they're already dead
         as fate and earth can will it – as all flesh is dead at birth)
                         but he

              who must set the cogs in motion, pauses
a kestrel that mounts air's summit without diving,
wary of the still field he must break

                  to draw blood
and make home.
        He cocks his musket, one eye closes;
all creation hackles, that last instant, at the catch
of metal brushing back upon itself, gathered to spring.
     There will be no undoing
       the spark that follows.

Alien

…apparently General-of-the-Army Prince Rupert's bluecoats, stood their ground and repulsed all attacks; one eyewitness said "they (the bluecoats) were like a wall of brass." Eventually, Lord-general Thomas Fairfax led his Regiment of Foot and his Regiment and Lifeguard of horse against them from all sides.

David C. Wallace, Twenty-Two Turbulent Years 1639 - 1661

Captain, sure, the field is falling.

Well, boy, we'll stand a while and watch it go.

Why do our ones run so fast?

Those who would overthrow the will of God are swift of foot

And come on like the rain – best to stay dry.

But why do we stay still?

Because, lad, there's a price for those

Who call Eire their mother but who brave the sea

To fight where they are called.

No prison cell of theirs will hold us,

But the hanging tree.

So then I'll meet my maker here or there?

This field before you is the last you'll gaze upon

So drink it in, boy, and thank all the stars

Your boots stay on the earth.

Then I'd best brush my coat.

Not long till they come now, sir. They look sore afraid.

There's none more frightening than us

With nothing left to fear.

I'll stand. But, captain, if I quake

'tis only that the wind blows awful fierce.

Yes, lad, I know. I feel it too.

Slope

This is how you map the ground.
There is a hill. There, the valley intersects two ridges
where the river forces its way through.
You can trace the contours of the land tree by tree
but that means nothing to a body in flight
looking for the best way his legs can carry him.

Here is where gravity takes over:
to the North, a ridge,
to the South a beck that you might cross
to the East the long field and the coming night
blurred with the onset of snow. West is your best way
of tracing how it went, but some things go unwritten

for example, how, if you try running it,
the sky is veined with rocking twigs,
and how your soul's larvae-like container betrays itself
under a metal case it can't live up to, tongue furred,
heart bursting, every joint's acid wail against gravity
the only measure of gradient.

This is what draws us back each time -
the miles between which can't be charted
save that, here, man knew what it is to be hunted
and to hunt without the comfortable bulk of machinery
to distance things; an iron cloy tinges the soil's bowels
and the ground falls away.

Malfosse

Cut first and gain a moment more.
They didn't tell him how the soul wells up
inexorable as a wave

in the eyes of the one opposite;
he's pissed himself, and still he stands and snarls
cut first and gain a moment more

the trapped badger facing down
a mongrel cur that's been whipped from behind,
one swell in an ocean of flesh.

There is complicity in this rage;
he knows without it his pike arm would falter -
cut first and gain a moment more

or else you might remember
that you don't know why you're standing here
wind-tossed, half-drowned with muck -

and so he roars, inexorable as a wave rising,
to breach that wall so fear won't dash him into flotsam.
Cut first. The mud sucks, bides its time.

Palm Sunday

For days on end the rain had mizzled on, swelling the stunted beck. As the people were stirring, darker tendrils were seen fingering their way downstream; around the washing place, the mud took on a clayish hue. Dim thunder rolled further up the valley.

8am:

It was around this time that the village women noticed a pinkish foam spewed on the banks, slurrying the light crust of snow. The current gushed rusty as old nails, and had the same smell. They resigned themselves to washing the next day.

11am

The water turned the colour of garnets, and grew sticky. Some tried to boil it, but the taint wouldn't bleach away. Whispers were heard of a second coming.

2pm:

From overhead, the swollen river almost seemed to bloom, a gash running through the pale limb of the valley. Dogs puked wetly in the sodden meadows where they drank from it. One girl who slipped wore the resulting stains all her life.

5pm

Clotted weeds festered, tangled together like sacrificial virgins' hair. Trout underbellies gleamed in their dark mass, and the limp ribbons of eels wound themselves around each clump. Frogspawn glared, red-eyed, through the stricken rushes.

8pm:

The torrent stuttered on into the dark, a sluggish pulse that wouldn't leave be, though all around it choked. In the houses people listened wide-eyed, gazing into nothing like sheep before a storm. At the crossing place, a bridge of bodies juddered.

The Field of Souls

There is nothing between the one stark tree on the ridge,
cupping the moon as a pedestal,
and the moss-pocked flanks of the stone obelisk
couched in its throne of holly bush.

Nothing but the sky's bowl, brimming, its ouija tilt
against the fields' crazed patchwork,
the woven byways of the hedgerows holding in
each new year's tribute.

A warbler sings. Wind-scythed, soft miles of wheat heads
dip and right themselves
turning their faces in an onslaught of silver
as if waves of fleeing souls

still brushed against them, stumbling desperately
towards the lower ground.
Soon harvest time will bring its reckoning again,
cutting them loose

and then there will then be nothing in between
the tree and the stone obelisk
except the heavy sky, brooding, a legacy of stubble
and the warbler's cry.

The Welsh Hirelings

The roads by which they entered were little trodden
as few left the marches and valleys then
not knowing the savagery of the plains as such
but given to repeating what the bards told them
of the smooth lands with their smoother tongues
and sharpened words for not belonging

until the Fair Unknown, a dragon prince
heard the valley's loose limbed syllables cry forth
a hollow song whose past had not concerned him
before it was of use, ignited their lords with his belly fire,
and reserves fattened deep around the heart fretted
with the tug of flatter lands to trample.

One by one they will slip back to hollow coombes
which birthed them, not when the mouth of Hell,
the dank field, has breathed upon and spat some out
but once they feel the shackles round their tongues
tightening fast, cold at the root and shrunken in,
the way with words begin to leave them.

After Battle

The dead king lay, sprawled limbs a ballad
told to the impressionable mud
so quick to cling and smother martyrs,
the hill's lip pouted with his blood.

The monks muttered behind their hands -
it was a stupid place to build.
*An abbey needs flat ground, so what
if it's not quite where he was killed?*

The live king, though, would not back down -
he knew there was no way in hell
to take the dead king's place, except
to sanctify the spot he fell.

So, slowly, the foundations climbed
(though extra columns were required
to prop up all the overhang
where wall went on but hill expired)

till finally the work was done -
arched gracefully, the abbey stood
washed in the evening's honeyed light,
framed by an emerald crown of wood.

The conqueror went straight to mass,
gave thanks he was now in the Right,
and prayed to make the country great
and that he'd win all future fights,

but the dead king lay under stone
through years incessant as the tides
quietly going back to earth,
not minding that his God changed sides.

Night Light

As the gleam shalloped
      wavering

  a split apricot

behind rain's sparse curtain at the window

    when no other sign of destiny

came to announce itself

   who lingered by it

       wakeful, working or loose-ended?

Two making love

  (after all these fey lights are most kind to bodies

  glibly pretending not to be bodies)

or making war

     across a long expanse of table?

 Whichever one

   2am and summer

      even at their fullest

cannot stop it.

Notes

The Forgotten
The law stating that all able-bodied males over 14 should do two hours of longbow practice every week supervised by local clergy was never, apparently, repealed.

The Crow
Corvus corvus, the Latin name for crow, has a very solemn ring to it. There is already a famous English folk ballad called 'The Three Ravens', which is about birds discussing the merits of various knights slain in combat as their next meal. It is a gruesome, but oddly lyrical and fascinating poem; the themes are all to do with faithfulness, how the dead are remembered, and how, whatever its history, the body is only a temporal object made of meat.

Stubble Dreams
Many battlefields are now put to use as arable land, and the cut stalks in summertime take on a new poignancy when you consider what happened all those years ago. It is very easy to impose a sense of 'presence' or put words into imaginary dead mouths.

He
William the Conqueror's other unofficial title was 'William the Bastard', and he did, in fact, use the tactic of feigned retreat to win the Battle of Hastings. He later went on to raid the north of England mercilessly.

At the Watershed
Watershed: an area or ridge of land that separates waters flowing to different rivers, basins or seas, and, being naturally lush, is an ideal location for combat. The area of the Midlands where Naseby and Bosworth are situated is one such place.

Facts of Life
Anyone who has been in combat seems to say the same, that everything you know or believe shrinks down to staying alive

Hymn for the Dawn
The tension just before combat is hard to imagine, looking at a time when Hell was treated as a universal fact rather than a supposition. Prayers before battle were part of the necessary preparations; Richard III famously had trouble organising mass on the day of his death.

The Ambush
Parliamentarian Colonel Okey fired the first shots at the Battle of Naseby; he led the initial ambush on the Royalist army from a side position behind Sulby Hedges.

Alien
Prince Rupert's Bluecoat regiment included many foreign Catholics, including Irishmen and Spaniards. At Naseby, they earned a fearsome reputation; this suicidal courage had equally grim origins - they knew that, if captured, the Parliamentarians would treat them as a threat to English sovereignty and hang them on the spot.

Slope
One large, steep area at Towton, where hundreds of fleeing Lancastrian troops were slaughtered running downhill, is still nicknamed 'The Bloody Meadow.'

Malfosse
Malfosse ('evil ditch') was where the Saxons supposedly made their last stand against the Normans at Hastings, and is said to be depicted briefly in the Bayeux Tapestry. The ground around the area is extremely marshy.

Palm Sunday
After the Battle of Towton, which was fought on Palm Sunday, so many corpses fell into the Cock Beck at the crossing that soldiers ended up using their comrades' bodies as a bridge. Some chroniclers claimed that the river ran red for days afterwards.

The Field of Souls
The ridge where the battle of Towton was fought, along with its stone monument, is surrounded by lush wheat fields. When the wind blows. the sudden waves of silver have a hypnotic effect.

The Welsh Hirelings
Welsh troops and support were a key part of the victory at Bosworth. Henry VII was a cunning propagandist, who used his heritage, prophecies of a hero who would free Britain from the English and the Red Dragon emblem – long believed to have been the battle standard of King Arthur – to marry his own cause to that of Wales.

After Battle
The new King William insisted that Battle Abbey be built on the hilltop where King Harold fell, despite all advice to the contrary. At one point the monks overseeing the construction even tried to move it without telling him, only to be soundly rebuffed. You can see from the ruin just how complex the foundations had to be in order to support it.

Night Light
There's no escaping the fact that all conflicts begin with ordinary conversations and plans in a domestic setting. One wonders how many lighted windows at 2am might conceal something of a far greater magnitude than we imagine...